Sunbeams and other coincidences

Lily Buchanan

Sunbeams and other coincidences © 2022
Lily Buchanan

All rights reserved.

No part of this publication may be reproduced, stored in a retrieval system, or transmitted, in any form or by any means, electronic, mechanical, photocopying, recording or otherwise, without the prior written permission of the presenters.

Lily Buchanan asserts the moral right to be identified as author of this work.

Presentation by *BookLeaf Publishing*

Web: www.bookleafpub.com

E-mail: info@bookleafpub.com

ISBN: 978-93-5744-429-3

First edition 2022

DEDICATION

To Jessica

who doesn't want to be mentioned, but here we
are.

I'm so glad I don't have to be pretty and blonde
to be your best friend.

To him (you know who you are)

without whom I would not have been okay with
it all falling apart.

I did go there, I found the compromise and look
what came out of it.

ACKNOWLEDGEMENT

I have so many people in my life without whose influence I never would have dared to dream about this book being in your hand. It would be impossible to thank everyone on a single page and although you'd all deserve it, I cannot mention all of you. Please know, you all have my eternal gratitude.

I'd like to thank BookLeaf Publishing, without whom this book would never have existed. Thank you for giving me the chance to be a published poet.

I'm also very grateful for my parents and brother. Without them I wouldn't be who I am today. I'm very thankful that you permitted me to read as much as I wanted when I was little and for building me a new shelf every time I run out of space for new books.

A huge thank you to Jessica, my dearest friend turned proof reader. I couldn't have pulled it off without you. You said I could do it and it turns out you really are always right.

I'd like to express my gratitude to Mr. Geenen, my favourite English teacher in high-school, who complimented me on my writing ever so often and whose constructive criticism always stuck with me. (I apologise for any errors you've encountered, but I assure you they were most likely intentional).

I'd like to thank all the people who tried to bring me down. Thank you so much for getting me my dreams.

To end with a cliché: thank you, dear reader. Thank you for buying this book and keeping poetry alive.

Backyard travels

Are you crying?

No.

Yeah, guys, she's definitely crying.

No, I'm not crying.
I am raging.
I am
I am
I am a million words in my head.
Distressed like a monkey who has just been
snatched from its forest home.
Rattling the bars of its diamond cage,
knowing full well it is unbreakable.

I am eloquent.
Not when waterfalls of seawater
fall down from the way I see the world
and turn my cheeks
into salt flats.
Why travel the world to see those
when the opinions of other people
can create them in your own backyard?

Bareface Oscar goes to...

It must be amazing
Being an actor
Going to work bareface every day
Knowing exactly what you'll become
as soon as the brushes start touching your face
as someone starts combing your hair.
All colours and softness, finger waves and wax.

I don't need all that.
I go bareface every day
and I'm still someone I'm not
on a day to day basis.
The Oscar should go to me.

Miss you most

There are lots of days when I miss you most.
And every time I think I won't be able to miss
you more
than I already do.
Those are the days, when dreaming about you
isn't enough,
but not dreaming about you is simply
impossible.

Mustard

I didn't say
I love you
first.

You might already have said it three
four
times before I said it back.

The details are foggy.

I remember wanting to know how those words
would taste.
If they'd roll off my lips like sweet honey.
Stick to my tongue
or
bounce off my teeth.

Instead, they tasted like mustard.
Sharp
zingy
but interesting all the same.

Your lies tasted like chocolate ice cream.
Sweet and all too easy
to swallow.

But darling,
didn't you know
that ice cream and mustard
don't mix?

Concrete pavement

I am not in love with the plant that grows
through the cracks in the pavement.
They call it strong.
They call it exceptional.
They call it a natural miracle.

They talk about it poetically.
Like it chose to grow in the worst circumstances
by choice.
Like it chose to be strong.
Like it chose to be exceptional.
As if it doesn't wish for soft sand and copious
amounts of water every day.
Standing alone.
Enduring nature's ceaseless ruthlessness.

Some feel like that plant all the time.
Craving their morning coffee
while desperately clawing their roots further into
the ground
trying to not fall off the earth's surface
and barely succeeding.

Call this strong.
Call this exceptional.
Call this a natural miracle.

Guitar

Sunday morning
You're not here
But if you were
you would probably be playing

A guitar
with some strings a little too loose
and some a little too tight
to sound on key

Your beautiful fingers
softly pulling those strings
your elbow lightly resting
on its body

Take me back to the days
where I didn't need to be jealous
of the way your hands
caressed its neck

Your fingers brushing my skin
just as delicately
while I trembled
as those strings

Off key
with entangled hands
we wrote our own story
the most beautiful symphony of all

Missing

I've been putting up posters
on every corner of every street
on every lamppost I could find

Missing person
Male
6 ft. tall
Dark hair
  or maybe blonde?
Eyes: blue
  or green?
  or brown?
Last seen: walking around in my mind
  or on some screen?
  or in my dreams?
  or maybe on the corner of this street?

Please call me
if you see him

You told me

You told me
saying I love you
wasn't enough

I told you
"if I show you
how I love you
you'll leave"

You told me
"I won't"

I struck the match
and burned our city down
to show you
the blaze of my love was more radiant
than the flaming sun

If you'd asked me
I would have burned the world down
if only to show you the light

You left

The lonely handkerchief

There's a little handkerchief
in my drawer.
Pristine and white,
lace around its edges.
It lies there,
in between my socks
and my knitted sweaters.

My little handkerchief
is a prima ballerina,
perfect between the everyday greyish ones
with its lace tutu and my embroidered initials.

It's not to be used
on dreary days
when the grey ones
get stained with tears.

But it gets a little jealous
in its drawer world
where all the socks
are stacked in pairs
and all the sweater sleeves
wrap around each other.

Embracing a single tear
might be less lonely.

Lips

I've been killing my lips over you for weeks.
Each piece of skin diverting,
from a we, that will never be an us.
Each drop of blood,
nothing more than a reminder,
that I must still be alive inside.

Ugly

The first time they called me ugly,
was in first grade.
The person who said it had been in my class for
almost 3 years.
Her words still rolled off me,
like raindrops roll off a bird's feathers.

Being ugly, for me, meant being unkind,
being mean.
The Disney cliché of being ugly on the inside.
I still believed in fairy tales.
To them, it meant something else,
something visible and tangible.
And to them, that was something so much worse
than just being unkind.

The second time they called me ugly,
was in second grade.
The person who said it, was not alone anymore,
and the second time soon became a third, a
fourth.
Their words were no longer a single raindrop,
but my umbrella of feathers was still strong.
But as the tide comes in,
there's not much an umbrella can do.

I stopped counting.

The I don't know how manieth time they called
me ugly,
ugly had gotten many names, but they all meant
the same.
"Not good looking."
The feathers had started bending, breaking,
words were pouring in.
And though I no longer believed in fairy tales,
these words seemed the ultimate truth.
The only truth that mattered.

If you tell the bird it's not a bird long enough,
will it stop believing it can fly?

In high school I discovered there were even
more "uglies".
"Not pretty."
"Too smart for your own good."
"Teachers pet."
Having other priorities than eyeliner and the
latest gossip,
were like sin.

The church I grew up in,
had taught me to value other things in life.
It taught me to work hard,
to be friendly,
and to always help others in need.

My church didn't have cold stone walls of
"which foundation are you wearing today?"
My baptism wasn't with face wash and night
cream.
My sermons consisted of "How was school
today?" and "It sucks you got an F on a test you
worked SO hard for."
My holy scripture was my diary, in which I
neatly wrote down all my homework and test
results.
It were not my gods screaming at me at the top
of their lungs,
that I could be a perfect person on the inside,
but I would still burn in their hell for not looking
cute.

At some point I must have chosen to believe
them.
The compassionate sound of my gods drowned
out by millions of raindrops and the high tide of
despair.
Propaganda for the people ugly on the inside.
Witch hunt for the people ugly on the outside.

When the idea of the cage is real enough,
the bird WILL forget how to fly,
and no matter how hard it tries,
its wings will never be the same again.

Sunny Instagram pictures

He had been travelling
around the world.
Chasing the sun
like it was the love of his life.
People call him brave and free.

The longer the days
The shorter the nights.
To be in sunlight
means to not be in the dark.
To not be a captive of his own thoughts.

He did not care for the beauty of Greenland
nor was he awed by the vastness of Australia
He was not afraid of monsters or ghosts
that roam the darkness.
His running thoughts were always more sinister.

The pitch-black of a moonless night
could not match the shadow
he was desperately running away from
in his own mind.
but emphasized it all the same.

Oh well,
at least he had
pretty Instagram pictures
filled with sun.
Wouldn't we all love to be him?

Lie to me some more

Do you remember
the night we got stuck on the side of the road
with a broken down car
and an even more broken us?

We went stargazing
to not waste the night
and drank booze from the bottle
that was meant as a gift.

When we watched the falling stars
we didn't judge them for falling
but rather made silent wishes
for the night to never end.

I asked you
are we over for you?
As much as we are over for me?
Even though I had never wanted us to end.

It's okay to lie to me some more
it's not like you haven't done that before.

You

I'm looking at you,
lying in front of the crackling open fire.
I'm thinking about you.

If there were any words to describe you,
they'd be:
beautiful,
soft, sometimes fierce,
but always conveying warmth to the hearts of
others,
even if you're not really there.

At night, I miss you.
I think of you.
I dream of you.

But in the morning,
sitting in my garden,
I look at you again.
How you play among the leaves.
How you walk along the garden path.

And when I take my eyes off you for only a
moment,
I can feel your gentle smile on my face.
My dearest,
my most beautiful,
light.

Don't tell me it's a lie, only because you don't like the truth

Did you know
an autumn leaf
can have more
nuances than your
opinion on someone
you have met
3 seconds ago?

Cold air

We met on a winter day.
Cold air, no clouds, bright sun.
Curtains closed.
God on hold.

You were hiding under my bed.
Cold air, soft pillows, warm blankets.
Eyes open.
Sight on hold.

I was just tired of feeling.
Cold air, cold words, you said,
it's okay.
Feelings on hold.

We said some kind of goodbye on a winter day.
Cold air, no clouds, bright sun.
Heart open.
Demons on hold.

A letter to my Star

My dearest, dearest Star
you came into this universe
with no expectations of your own.
Your cloud of dust around your
like a cosy blanket.

Your parents
moon and sun
opposites attracted
and there you were.

From that moment on
you'd be my Star.
Your radiant starlight
in no way inferior
to Castor's or Pollux's.

Beauty unparalleled
bringing joy to whoever
lays eyes upon you
stars and planets alike.

The galaxy isn't always
a beautiful place.
The Milky Way can seem
dark and cold.
Some days you won't be
radiant or gleeful.
But I promise you
you will be loved
always.

The notch in your bedpost

I bet you're tired
of hearing about depressed girls
who w(h)ine and dine
in candlelit rooms.

Their lives golden
speckled with the occasional shadow
but never looking
any less than bronze.

Their hearts buzzing
like crickets who wished
they could call it a night
without being afraid.

Drinking gin mixed with
lighter fluid
swallowing lit matches
to feel warm inside.

But the only ones
who deserve the flames
are the ones
who hung the ropes.

So if you're tired
of hearing them cry
holding on to bedposts
that aren't theirs

choking themselves
on the ropes
they did not hang
for themselves

maybe you shouldn't
have broken them.

Thin walls

"Some people want to reach the moon
but you conquer mountains by getting up in the
morning.

You don't realise how much your lips
are deserving of the kisses I want to give you
every day.

Your mind is like a shrine
I want to fall asleep at, worshiping you
every night.

How often did I wish
my eyes were one way mirrors
so you could gaze straight into my soul
and find a home in mine, like I do in yours.

If perfection is made up of trials and errors
endings and beginnings
you'd think you would have recognised it
when it was staring you straight in the face."

I heard her say to him
through the thin walls of the hotel room
next to mine.
And all I could think was:
how does she know how I love?

Life stories

They declared it a book,
like we needed a hard cover,
like that would prevent us from tearing out
our own pages of fear and doubt.

Secret ode to the future wife of Daniel

Once upon a time
there lived a fantastic woman
who didn't believe
she deserved to have the world.

Her days were fairy tale filled
and riddled with ghostly lights.
She sometimes called herself cheap
but I've never known anyone who was more like
champagne.

Once a man called her floozy
and she looked him dead in the eye
silent and graceful
with a look, I swore, could have moved a
mountain.

When she laughed, I laughed.
When she cried, I cried.
And when she got her distant dreams of Daniel
there was only one inside joke I could think of…

Fire brigade.